THE AMERICAN POETRY REVIEW/HONICKMAN FIRST BOOK PRIZE

The Honickman Foundation is dedicated to the support of projects that promote spiritual growth and creativity, education and social change. At the heart of the mission of the Honickman Foundation is the belief that creativity enriches contemporary society because the arts are powerful tools for enlightenment, equity and empowerment, and must be encouraged to effect social change as well as personal growth. A current focus is on the particular power of photography and poetry to reflect and interpret reality, and, hence, to illuminate all that is true.

The annual American Poetry Review/Honickman First Book Prize offers publication of a book of poems, a $3,000 award, and distribution by Copper Canyon Press through Consortium. Each year a distinguished poet is chosen to judge the prize and write an introduction to the winning book. The purpose of the prize is to encourage excellence in poetry, and to provide a wide readership for a deserving first book of poems. *Likenesses* is the nineteenth book in the series.

LIKENESSES

Likenesses

Heather Tone

The American Poetry Review

Philadelphia

Cover photo: Riley Buttery, from her *Sasha II* series
Book design and composition: VJB/Scribe
Distribution by Copper Canyon Press/Consortium

Library of Congress Control Number:

ISBN 978-0-9833008-3-0 cloth
ISBN 978-0-9833008-2-3 paper

9 8 7 6 5 4 3 2 FIRST EDITION

CONTENTS

AN ATTEMPT AT AN INTRODUCTION — STRAP YOURSELF IN

Blooming asters on hillsides look like boys.

The boys look like stars breaking up …

Carolyn Forché once said something to the effect that it is impossible to write about any one thing without it transforming into something else — this is the quicksilver nature of this material we call "language." Octavio Paz said something to the effect that metaphor is one of the great discoveries (inventions?) for precisely this reason — metaphor is a way to contain — no, not contain — *acknowledge,* the essential instability of life. We are all propping each other up, all living in houses made of cards, what we think of as a self is really multiple, as Whitman knew.

Likenesses is made up of five sequences of poems, many of which use the engine of simile to drive them forward. Running alongside this simile-generating machine, there is something also here of Genesis — the book is, in part, an origin myth, an attempt to create the world by naming it. Imagining another poet, Jorie Graham captured this spirit:

Frank O'Hara, wandering around New York naming everything he can,
as if he is going to make New York City finally really exist.

Heather Tone is in Frank O'Hara's tribe, in that part of her project — joyful, playful, unsettling, brilliant — is to name everything she can, except that now it's too late in the game to imagine that whatever is named could simply *be,* without at the same time being — *becoming* — something else. Or many somethings elses, infinite many. In this way, these poems suggest, we are all connected. Thich Nhat Hanh calls it *interbeing,* how everything exists only in relation to everything else. But these poems embody this idea, not merely enact it. This embodiment happens in real time, the time it takes to read them, as one thing transforms, word by word, into another thing — *Sun marries clouds and creates a crown.* How we are transformed, reading them, how this transformation serves to remind us that we are all connected:

All you have to do is consider where you

would be without other people …

Another of the myriad pleasures here in these pages is to witness a mind in the act of dis-covery—the poems find themselves, and then turn to dust, over and over, until it becomes clear that the process of finding the poems *is* the poem.

The maple tree looks like a woman. The cotton-

wood looks like an old man....

. . . .

... Perhaps, at a certain point, it would

be wise to ask yourself why you're doing

this....

Perhaps, at a certain point, all artists (perhaps all human beings), need to ask themselves why they are doing this, whatever *this* is—this feels like a prerequisite for being conscious, though these poems have their roots in the subconscious dream realms, where all art begins.

Theodore Rozewicz, the great post-war Polish poet, has a poem that some of these sequences echo—in it a speaker tries vainly to slow the world down by naming it, by being precise, by reducing the world to the essentials, yet the world cannot be contained, simply our place in it guarantees that whatever it is that causes our eyes to land on this rather than that, to imagine you rather than her, begins to leak out around the edges.

Here's a bit from Rozewicz's "In the Middle of Life":

After the end of the world
after my death
I found myself in the middle of life
I created myself
constructed life
people animals landscapes

this is a table I was saying
this is a table

on the table are lying bread a knife
the knife serves to cut the bread
people nourish themselves with bread

one should love man
I was learning by night and day
what one should love
I answered man

Like Rozewicz, Tone reads, at times, as slightly dissociated, as if the narrator were walk-ing away from a war or trauma, now and newly unsure of each step. The syntax here is mea-sured, without fireworks, as if the act of uttering were enough, as if each thing encountered simply needed to be named in order to be sure it still exists. Jung posited that dissociation might be a natural response to the weirdness of being alive, the acknowledgment that we are multiple, fragmented, broken. We are, each of us, after all and in fact, walking away from a war. With Tone, unlike Rozewicz, all possibilities flood each moment.

Likenesses is divided into five sequences, each of which speaks, or completes, or compli-cates, the sequence that come before — in this way the structure of the book mirrors a cause and effect structure (the broken cup on the floor must come after the full cup on the edge of table). The section titled "Likenesses" becomes complicated by "Gestures." A character (antihero) is introduced. We try again. It cannot last.

The last sequence is "Disintegration: Poems for Eliot" — *Eliot* is:

George Eliot suggests, "We all of us, grave or light, get our thoughts entangled
in metaphors, and act fatally on the strength of them."

And so, all these transformations, all this instability, though handled lightly, contains something of life and death — the deep instability of the project, and thereby of life itself, seeps into us.

Earlier (about 800 words ago) I floated the concept of *interbeing*, but these poems do not merely *enact* this idea, they *embody* it. This is what I mean: I could feel, in my body, while reading them, the inherent instability of what we call *living*. This being alive thing is, when you think about it, when you are in the presence of a poet who is fearless, just fuckin' weird. Some art makes me believe, or tricks me into believing, that it is eternal, when really noth-ing is. Sometimes a song appears and it is as if it was always there, waiting to be found, con-taining an essence of what feels like inevitability. Enacting is a game for those who cling to narrative, to the story they've been telling. Strap yourself into this book, allow yourself to ride it all the way to the top — remember: *At a certain point it would be wise to ask yourself why you are doing this.*

— Nick Flynn

As for foam … it appears to lack any usefulness; then its abundant, easy, almost infinite proliferation allows one to suppose there is in the substance from which it issues a vigorous germ, a healthy and powerful essence, a great wealth of active elements in a small original volume. Finally, it gratifies in the consumer a tendency to imagine matter as something airy, with which contact is effected in a mode both light and airy, which is sought after like that of happiness either in the gustatory category (foie gras, entremets, wines), in that of clothing (muslin, tulle), or that of soaps (film-star in her bath). Foam can even be the sign of a certain spirituality, insomuch as the spirit has the reputation of being able to make something out of nothing…

— ROLAND BARTHES, *MYTHOLOGIES*

I clothe one in flowers. I clothe him in flowers. I cover one with flowers. I cover him with flowers. I destroy one with flowers. I destroy him with flowers. I injure one with flowers. I injure him with flowers.

I destroy one with flowers; I destroy him with flowers; I injure one with flowers: with drink, with food, with flowers, with tobacco, with capes, with gold. I beguile, I incite him with flowers, with words; I beguile him, I say, "I caress him with flowers. I seduce one. I extend one a lengthy discourse. I induce him with words."

I provide one with flowers. I make flowers, or I give them to one that someone will observe a feastday. Or I merely continue to give one flowers; I continue to place them in one's hand, I continue to offer them to one's hands. Or I provide one with a necklace, or I provide one with a garland of flowers.

— FROM "OFFERING FLOWERS," *TECHNICIANS OF THE SACRED*, ED. JEROME ROTHENBERG

LIKENESSES

Likenesses

When he is dead, a man in a

bathing suit looks most like a little boy.

A woman in a bathing suit

looks like a woman, unless she is quite

thin, in which case she looks like a little boy.

A little girl in a sundress looks like a little boy

in a sundress. Her mouth is a cold oval, as cold

as a strawberry. When dead, a robin redbreast

looks like a little girl, while it goes without

saying that Robin Hood looks like a boy.

The snowfield cresting the mountain looks

like a little girl sleeping on the mountain.

The pines, boys right before they disappear

into men with cold faces who carry hatchets.

Just before it dies, a car looks like a teenager, but only

if it was built before the '90s. After that, cars look like women.

Blooming asters on hillsides look like boys.

The boys look like stars breaking up.

When it is dead or just before, an ant looks like

a woman sunning herself on a beach.

Crabs look like little girls playing hopscotch.

Grasshoppers look like middle school boys

throwing bugs at girls in late summer.

Spoons are the eyes of women asleep behind rainstorms.

Their interlaced fingers look like two children afflicted with dwarfism.

The pint glass is a man preparing to dive off a tall building.

Paper planes look like little girls in skirts, real planes are women.

When it is dead, a fox has the eyes of a little girl.

A faun looks like a little boy, its bones like a courtyard full of children.

When it is alive the plant, which is called kinnikinnick,

looks like a woman. It covers the floors of forests, its berries

shining wetly like the eyes of a living fox.

When it is dead, it looks like an old man in rags sinking into the earth.

A stump looks like a tombstone out in the middle of the forest.

It's easy: just close your eyes and think of a thing. Does it look

more like a little girl or a little boy?

Words look like dead prostitutes, twisted, thin: my subjective opinion.

If it is alive, a dog looks like a plump cloud or a stringy cloud.

If it is a different kind of dog, it is a slightly worn shoe.

If it is a different kind of dog still, it is perhaps dead.

A bluebird looks like a woman frozen in water.

A hay bale looks like a king who died in his sleep one September.

A dried cornstalk, a dead prince.

The country church looks like a little boy.

The city school looks like a pyramid of boys.

Driving by it reminds me of the House of Windsor.

A computer looks like a man killed in his prime

by a heart attack. A chair looks like a shy little

girl made of blue plastic. The stuffed red dog looks

like a little boy. The "Welcome" sign looks like a grave.

The novels look like fat babies, broken teeth.

The lamps look like young women of fashion.

Paperclips look like little boys. Staples look like

little boys. Rubber bands look like boys.

Some citizens of some countries never have enough

to eat. Scissors look like teenage boys, while knives

always are treasonous queens. Framed photographs look

like old women with plates of cookies. Calendars

with pictures of beautiful insects look like little girls.

Boys of a certain age look like parts are missing.

The window is a woman's eye measuring a certain horizon.

The man working at the restaurant looks like

a little girl in a pinafore. He has that androgynous

look that is popular right now. A wine glass

looks like a woman. The chalkboard with

specials looks like a teenage girl, looks like

how she is when she wears red lip gloss out

to see a band. The drummer looks

like a little girl wasting away. The key

lime pie looks like a man. The man travels

to Florida in a pastel-colored polo shirt.

Croissants are women wrapped in gauze

sitting for paintings. Peach pie

is a little girl in a pinafore. The painter

tries to infuse the dead with life, much

like vodka may be infused with roses or bacon.

A vase of asters looks like a vase of little boys.

The entrees look like women waiting to be taken.

All you have to do is consider where you

would be without other people. The green

lawn would become a man. If you are a man,

the swimming pool will become a woman,

cool and perfumed, with blonde highlights in her

hair. The swimming pool, in fact, looks like a

woman now, reflects several of them so that

the cool, blue women are drowned. When

drowned, such women resemble little boys.

The maple tree looks like a woman. The cotton-

wood looks like an old man. When all the trees

are saplings, they look like little boys

going barefoot. At a certain point, it would

be wise to ask yourself why you're doing

this. The man who walks under the cottonwoods

looks like an older version of himself:

long years have sanded him down to sinewy

essentials. That is to say that it will not

be much of an absence in space when he

disappears. The sun where he walks looks like

melted children. His white shirt looks like a woman

flinging out a handkerchief to pause the game.

An eagle looks like an old man. A flamingo

looks like a little girl with a crooked leg.

A parakeet looks like a woman on her way

to a luncheon, or looks like the decorative touch

to the woman's hat. A goose looks like a little boy.

A duck looks like a little boy. The duck is an

obstreperous fellow among crumbs, while the goose is a

boy savant, flying high and cold in perfect

V's of thought. The goose is more machine

than boy, I think. The bluebird looks like a

woman frozen in water. The sparrows

bouncing around the bread look like little

girls in braids and uniforms. The nuthatch looks lost,

like a little girl. All of the birds look alive, for the

time being. The flicker looks like an old carpenter

who drinks a few at the bar at the end of each day.

Most fairy tales are populated by little girls

and little boys. Little girls get stuck in towers

or turned to trees and little boys must use

their knives. Such delineations understand

the mind of the writer, to a degree. Rapunzel

looks like a little girl. Blue Beard's bride, a girl

with her smile knifed upon her. Snow White, however,

looks like a little boy, the center point around

which apples fall and arrows miss. (Arrows look

like boys sledding, while apples are women casting

off crowns of leaves.) Cinderella, too, looks like a little boy,

one on the cusp of self-sufficiency, her smock the color

of pepper. Her gloves look like the dirt wherein

she has dug. The garden around appears to be reaching

its hands toward her. Afternoon light lengthens

this lesson. A child turning pages has the look of a child.

The actor looks like a little boy. The actress

looks like a little boy. A candle looks like a

little girl with her arms held high in the milk-

light. Moths come near the light, as they do.

The moths look like 5th Avenue, where women

look like moths and moths look like

white gloves and gloves look like star

light eating up all the children's arms.

Gesture

Sometimes you cannot touch what you have done.

One morning I decided one word deserves extra attention.

I gestured to snow, and it piled thusly upon chimneys.

I gestured to foam, and it billowed forward as a flock of swans.

I gestured to the harbor, and it pressed the ocean out until it disappeared.

I gestured to the schoolyard, and kindergarteners were lifted in its black glow.

I gestured to the lawn adjacent, and it said it felt like a meadow.

I gestured to a meadow, and it gestured to the forest.

I gestured to the tree, and it gestured to a tree that was farther away.

I gestured to the print, and it froze the sentiment.

I gestured to sky. There was failed transfer, a broken blue.

I looked long and hard to see what I could make of the problem.

The light turned everyone's clothes a bit dusty.

I gestured to my handbag, and it wasn't there.

Joan Didion was there, and she handed me a napkin.

She also handed me a better version of my own life.

I gestured to my ring, and it did nothing different, though I felt different about it after that.

I gestured to myself, and you did nothing, but I felt exposed.

I gestured to the page, and it said it wanted me to care for it.

I didn't know how to care for it.

I felt like my lungs were filled with snow.

I felt like I wanted to speak or not to speak.

I didn't know what I felt when you gestured toward the first letter of my name.

Someone escorted me to a clerestory window.

It was kind of like Arizona, only not so scrubby and more white.

I gestured to the thing being built, and you could not tell me what exactly it was.

I gestured to myself, and you suggested I have unreasonable expectations.

I made note of that a person can actually climb up into the thing.

I gestured to the chariot.

I asked if I could take your picture.

"Nope" is not even a real word, you know.

I gestured — again — to all the art projects going on around here.

I noted that we don't call them "art projects" now that we're out of high school.

I gestured to the marching band's footprints in the frosted grass.

When I was younger, I secretly wanted to get lost in the woods so that, once I was found
    half-frozen but in good spirits (given the circumstances), I could be on TV.

I gestured to where I got lost.

I've established the ground rules for this dialogue, and now it's up to you to meet me.

I gesture to myself, and the valves of my heart don't close properly.

I'm referencing the valves of the heart now, not the heart itself.

I gestured to the test, and it said it addresses open heart surgery, among other topics.

I gestured to the wreck, and the diagnostics team reported that the car was red.

I was clear-eyed as melting snow.

Wheels spun like silver dollars.

A drug dealer came crawling out of the smoke.

A cowboy came crawling out of the smoke.

What are a drug dealer and a cowboy doing sharing a cigarette? I thought.

I gestured vaguely, and it was meant to communicate that I felt confused.

I gestured to the cowboy, and he said, "I need you to use your cowboy skills."

I gestured to the way we looked, all dressed up for the photograph.

I gestured to how dry everything was, how brittle.

You aren't supposed to smile at all in that situation.

The hotel restaurant, I think, was called Michel's.

Michel, Michel, Michel.

I gestured to myself, and I was just saying some stuff I thought of, hoping you'd use that sound to make your way toward me.

I gestured to myself, and you might not think I meant anything specific.

When I woke up this morning, there were two inches of snow, just like the news said.

I brushed it off my car. I made footprints that glittered around my car.

I gestured to the man carrying boxes out of an apartment.

The next gesture I made had a clear purpose.

He waved back at me, but he didn't stop to talk. It was still very snowy.

I gesture to the script, and it says that someone named Patricia is supposed to enter now.

That was my part. I played the star role of Patricia in a play we put on several years ago.

It was this thing we did, when we weren't too tired or hungry, when we got sick of talking about ourselves.

I gestured to the park, and a leaf-collection truck grinded a bunch of leaves into fall-colored powder.

I gestured toward the compact cloud that sped left, obscuring the sun.

A mini coupe sped left, too.

A series of dogs sped left.

I gestured toward the quick reflexes of the mailman.

I gestured to Rosalind Franklin, who discovered DNA.

One day, she was in her laboratory looking out when the idea sort of raked itself together inside her.

Inside of our arms, there is a series of bases and interstices, which make these sophisticated bracelets.

I don't know the scientific names, but we can be beautiful (inside our arms).

Nope, says someone.

Someone gestures toward a window.

This abundance of ours must be spent extravagantly on food or the arts or sex, the creation of a cabaret. I won't be held responsible for the consequences of thrift.

I gestured to the tornado, and it swallowed Ohio.

I gestured to the volcano, and it folded Hawaii.

I gestured to the earthquake, and it refused to comment.

I gestured to the tsunami, and it said it preferred to be called Valerie. It curled its lip in our direction.

The cabaret flashed a toothy grin.

Here is a place we could go, or here are some things we could prepare for supper, some lambs, a whole trout lifted from an ice-crowded rectangle, potatoes like softened stones.

Here are some lettuces, which I have called from the lost beds of spices.

Here is a round of cheese, which is courtesy of the sheep in the meadow.

Here is an apple, which had lain coiled among last autumn's leaves, windfall, red sail.

Here is vanilla, which you have broken with your fingers.

Here is a glass for you and a glass for me and the brief choir of them at twilight.

Here is an elbow on a table, a hand draped over a knife.

My heart was feral, insatiable. My hunger was.

I gestured to my hunger. I was hungry. I was not. I thought I was not. I grew hungrier as time went by. I grew so hungry I couldn't tell what I was. I grew so hungry I became secondary to my appetites. I became foam. I became snow. I became a signal. I felt guilty, knowing I had no real reason. I had no place for myself. In the end, I was very, very hungry. I was so hungry. It was a song or a spell.

As for me, I own a few things, one of which is a gathering of muscles. I put my left foot
down. I put my right.

I gestured to the cave, and it said it housed a goddess, or something close to it.

I gestured to the goddess. Her voice sounded like dried leaves, flaked paint. It blew off the
mountain.

I had been seeking advice. I didn't know what to do.

"You know how many Things I/ could do without. Things I could/ do."

Some courtships are conducted largely through letters.

Antihero

Poetry deserves an antihero. Let's call

him Quentin. No, let's don't. Let's call him the Kid,

or Victor, or Jack. Let's call him a pair of scissors

shimmering near a pile of paper. Let's call him

a man drowning himself in two inches of liquid.

Let's watch him pull his head up, fountain

water through his lips. Let him consider desire, body

dry as a Japanese lantern. Let him consider

deer coming through fog to come together

on a lawn. Let's watch him kidnap someone.

Let's watch him bring a 9 mm. Let it be light

out, then grey, then blue-black, then grey. Let's

watch him raise a tear-lit face off a pillow.

The apartment is as quiet as a ticking clock. The

apartment swallows minutes you can never regather.

Against all our expectations, our man can

identify a robin's song over the phone, a bird singing

on the other side of water. Let's watch him forget

to listen to the speaker as instead he listens to the bird.

Let's watch him wander through an apartment full

of boxes, pick up objects, turn them, set them back.

He strikes a fine figure in a seersucker suit.

Let's acquire one for him. It will be his costume

of sorts, but something he could also wear

for other occasions. Let's give him a girlfriend

named Melody. She's from the right side

of the tracks. She likes him for his antihero

ways: smoke bombs, paintball parties, trays

of hors d'oeuvres made from endangered fish.

He did the research, though. He is full of empathy

and second guesses. At the age of seven, he

wore a mermaid outfit for Halloween. He takes a sip

of water. (We watch, wait.) Let's give him a highball.

Scratch that. Let's give him whiskey, no rocks, straight.

Let's allow him to wish he were somewhere

else, somewhere full of wheat and space.

Outside I see things are condensing around

undergrads in the Midwest who claim they've

been roofied, who don't recall the mink of a midnight

kiss or Davey Jones or bearded mammoths of

the Pleistocene. Our antihero has been in the bathroom

for a while now, finishing the Sunday crossword. He won't

touch his notebook. He's draped a towel over

his computer. He will take a bike ride through Central Park.

Let's call him a candy wrapper, Baby Ruth plastic

blowing across any piece of asphalt in the United States.

Let's call him a garage sale. Let's upgrade, call him

a souped-up truck. Let's call him Jupiter or

Christopher, the man who wants to watch over you

with binoculars after he's crawled out a window into space.

The plan is to circle nothing with a circle

so that it becomes something, the brilliant zero

of falling asleep. Today, the idea of God

is thin as grass-blade: it is our antihero who

makes or unmakes the world, whose every

smoke ring looks like a staring eye.

Gloria: a room letting in clouds, a man who

has no mother. Wherever he goes, roses melt

right off their stems. Wherever he goes,

corridors of lethal gas, last pages torn from books.

This is off-color Technicolor, the opposite

of Julie Andrews. With his power finger, he

draws a lazy oval and sits back as the screen

simply switches to a concrete-colored sweatshirt.

Let's call him fire damage or smoke damage. It's

unclear which is which after everything is gone.

I have a mind to say to you that I am here even

though my body is missing. Let's put him

in a classroom and see how he responds to

student inquiry. Let's make him a vegetarian.

He's the type who won't even eat honey.

Let's buy him season tickets to any sport

whatsoever. Do you want to see a ball

unravel distances? Do you want to see the

players tack, fake, tack? My name is the Coach.

My name appears on occasion on billboards.

My antihero looks to me for prompts or guidance,

listens to a hidden earpiece, pleases his audience

with his understanding of geometry, Cracker Jacks.

While our antihero has a limited understanding

of robins, he has a firm grasp of the history

of drag racing. Let's watch him siphon gas

from someone's Mercedes. Let's watch him brake

at a roadside museum, eat some peanuts, fall asleep

next to glassed-in, glass-eyed diamondbacks.

Let's watch him flirt shamelessly with a teenage ticket

girl, then get dusty as he speeds away with open

windows. A police chase: that's what he needs.

Our man rolls cigarettes in his shirt sleeve,

but then he stops at a dive motel in the middle

of Iowa when he's too tired, just like everyone

else. His empty car becomes an oasis. It lets in night, haze,

the occasionally clarifying beams of passing vehicles. In the

same frame but farther off, a blonde star disintegrates.

Wanna know what? I trust him, my antihero.

He's climbing toward my window. Let's watch

the eloquence of his scrawny shoulders. He

offers his edges to the very light. He deserves,

certainly, an origin story, as (I think we

can agree) does everyone. Let's return to a time

of heroes: Captain America hunched over

a typewriter, the Green Lantern. The eyes we are

given depict bones behind clothes. Let's watch our lad—

Joshua, we called him then—count the number of turns

it took to wash his hands, tick off telephone poles

in groups of ten. There was no storm system

churning ahead, no radioactive insect. There

was no dead father, love spurned, no sinister

planet peeking from behind the sun. One morning,

after catching a few fish in a mountain lake and cooking

bacon, he just stood up, cracked his knuckles.

As I was saying, though, and not to obscure

the point: the antihero doesn't have a stake

in debates over words like "effulgence"

or "luminescence." What grows out of his

chest pocket is a hand grenade. Let's watch

him at the coast, grey ocean throwing itself

over grey rock. He considers lonesomeness,

aspects of it like pieces of a teenager's body.

Writing this way is wanting to fold one's self up,

launch it toward another, perhaps another decade.

Elizabeth Taylor? Nah. Well, maybe. But our lad

has leanings toward the soft tough, a neck that

aches for thin, gold chain. He thinks of

his favorite documentary, a retrospective look

at *Saturday Night Live*, the roller skate age

of Bill Murray, Dan Aykroyd, Chevy Chase.

He's appropriated someone, but he's unclear

who. He has the mind of a chess player, or at least

an appreciation of ivory bishops and onyx knights,

of strolling through equatorial midnight gardens,

slicing through density with his precision of recall.

Unusually candid, he tells of his childhood in Michigan.

He was small then, as small as a tombstone. These were

his exact words: *I was small as a tombstone.* He says he

was quiet as a silver locket. He took things apart, like

toasters and motorcycles. He took apart maple leaves

by removing their bodies. He removed buttons

from button holes, delicate ones shaped like

white hearts. Some tasks are more difficult

if you think about the exact mechanics of their

accomplishment. Our antihero also once read all of

Whitman during a stint in the hospital, in which his

celery-like legs were not very useful and not very obvious.

Today the antihero—Nathan, he is named—

breaks a mirror. Let's watch. He does it

intentionally, with a piece of cement

that's calved off a cracked-out wishing

well. Here's what's real: physicality reflected

back in pieces. Let's watch him collect it all,

all that physicality, those plunging, icy

triangles. His gloves: unreal, but tight

of weave. Surprise if thorns dig in, surprise

if a girl sleeps for days, a pinned beetle,

an absent prince. Surprise, I've been told,

the people, and you move them,

win them over. Our antihero, our dark

horse: we demand success. Let him complete

his mission barefoot, get the girl after

ripping off a few cans of WD-40, easy

as a bowl of grapes. Clouds with smooth

torsos replacing suns. Seasons like stones.

Once upon a time, the antihero thought

of writing a poem that ended with a wedding,

and then he thought of something

better: a cherry-red, '65 Chevy Corvair.

The antihero is a form of sadness, a form

of letting go. He pulls away from a sexual

encounter with a sticky torso, limp as a new

leaf. Compositionally speaking, we are

not the things we were a few minutes

ago, and he intuits this, a comfortless space,

stumbles toward the Internet, the next minute

veers off, can barely stand the thought

of responding to email. Coins in his pocket:

his pocket is full of full moons, useless

in today's economy. He squints regularly,

hoping to make the city a little unreal.

His preferred attire consists of a smoking

jacket, though smoking is a nasty habit,

and so he quit last July, just in time for

fire season, undergrowth having piled in pine

forests like shade, junk mail, bad poems.

Combinations

Sun marries clouds and creates a crown.

The crown marries the other crown.

In response, a saint marries a wheel or a stone.

This unity becomes a point of reference.

Today, we don't much go in for wheels and stones.

We go in for folk rock, coming-of-age stories, and other things of beauty.

We go in for food trucks and roller derby.

We go in for *Casablanca*, two-lane highways, Ambien.

Dusk comes up. A bridge marries itself to sky.

Clouds marry themselves. One cloud extends its arm.

The sky, it is said, married earth and then was eaten.

A spaceship travels across like a sigh.

Blue tin, blue dent.

At one point we were married, and it felt like a toy.

Some poorly made toys splinter under the weight of air.

Air married the toy and made it something hard to keep track of.

An apple married air and suddenly there were physics.

A picture on the wall lists to the left.

The framed woman marries a plate of apples.

She is married to the white moment before the fruit and the white moment after.

I am married to the habit of watching a presentation or the blue husk around a tree.

Young pilgrim, I offer you my shoes. I offer you summer camp.

One of the blonde-faced counselors has married himself to *Simon and Garfunkel*.

One of the merry chefs has married herself to the dinner triangle.

Sleeping bags are not sacred enough. Tabitha refuses to stop crying.

Window fans are married to wind, and to the green wind beyond.

Once again a Friendly Dog stations itself in this scene.

A vase marries a dead clutch of stems.

A footrace begins with the click of a gun.

A guy crashes the talent show with a polished saw, marries folksong to experimental noise.

The marriage of certain objects in the mouth means they appear next to one another on shelves in supermarkets.

The marriage of certain objects in bones means you go to the hospital.

The marriage of certain objects in bones means the bones bloom.

Too much blooming kills the heart.

The marriage of certain objects in the heart means you might be a good communicator.

The marriage of certain objects in the mind means we can conceive of a god.

Thoreau marries God to picking up sticks and putting them in piles.

I pick up sticks and put them in piles.

Tolstoy marries God to an empty bowl.

I watch the empty bowl.

Melville marries God to a blind man.

Emily Dickinson marries herself to silence, and she also marries herself to a bird.

I marry myself to silence.

I retract silence.

Silence makes me feel like I don't exist.

John Donne marries a devil, thinks the better of it, then marries God.

Half of it is about the perfect dinner and half is about death.

My neighbor douses his grass with gasoline.

Fire ants are killed. Fire ant bodies marry deep blue dirt.

Voices of birds marry thick blue air.

Stomachs of pastured animals marry the white want of winter.

If beasts have something to put their bodies to, then so do we.

Syria might be an option, or sorting out genius photography from dabbling in the digital age.

In barns across the west, hay goes cold like analog.

Lacking hay, barns just go cold.

My spine has gone cold married to the silver zipper.

Mirrors marry the faces to the faces. I can't shake this sad lean-to.

I can't shake the feeling that you're washing your hands somewhere.

My spine marries someone's torso. My spine imprints on someone else's skin. My spine
comes in contact with your torso, and my scoliosis makes an S.

Several of the things we do, we do under the auspices of the church.

Presentations give way to new presentations.

One hotel is married to the tradition of having ducks walk down a red carpet to a fountain.

One day a duck steps off the red carpet, puts a triangle on brown carpet, grows bold.

You know what happens next.

Little kids marry chaos, draw it after them like wagons, trail sticky fingers along the wall.

One young man marries the thought that he will become a mechanic.

His mind meets the gears like snow meets western fields.

Gears glow like letters or eyes.

It is hard to think of this young man and where he ends up.

Marrying you was no mistake. I was afraid. I was turning around to see all the way around me.

You said, "What difference will it make if we live here or there?"

You said, "My eyes feel I have been staring at the same page for too long."

We retracted the marriage.

You married someone else. Onlookers looked on to see if it would stick.

I search the radio for something besides static.

I marry the thought of snow coming down in western fields, of talismans looking out of the dark with faces like wolves.

The body was married to the underside of a truck, to grease, bolts, bottles of Michelob in the afternoon.

She'd married herself to the porch where the sun struggled.

Wheat struggled against the sun.

Hedges struggled against the sun.

The cat struggled to unroll itself, and yes, part of that was about sun.

In the gallery, I was finally understanding the tour guide.

Black with gold, he said, the struggle of empires.

Red married to orange, the struggle of dominance.

Gold married to silver, the struggle of a common currency.

Does it sound better to say "married to" or "married with"?

The gallery guide notes how lines in this or that painting lead the eye away.

Those lines end somewhere in the real world, he suggests.

This isn't about paintings anymore, is it?

It's about Henry VIII's quiet moments, when he let his mind wander off across the heaving kingdom.

A hat keeps brightness off the face when daylight plunges itself down.

You are not the first person to recognize the talismanic properties of a favorite hat.

You are not the first person to visit Yellowstone National Park.

You are not the first to be stilled by the mathematics of waves.

You are not the first to note how real everything is.

Jack pines marry the air. A thin-legged deer bends one knee. My friends and I gasp.

Somewhere in this country is an older literary movement.

A couple of cows gnaw the state line.

An axe marries the white chest.

Cutting down trees is something you read about rather than see.

What we marry is white.

Beyond this, there is a dust-covered beast straining under sunless sun.

What happens at the office radiates in wrists and eyes.

The dust beast rinses its mouth at the end of day, makes no more noise than moth or sleigh.

The trick here: don't make any sudden movements or say any sudden things.

Consider in the silence the bygone time when the dust beast put on its white cape.

White capes for heroes.

White capes for Kilimanjaro.

White capes for feast days.

It's taken me several years of thinking to even begin to think of this.

It's taken lots of turning around and lots of different settings.

Teenagers marry the feeling they have like they are a spell.

English credits emerge like baby eagles. Eaglets, they are called.

Their scruffy heads emerge and take up all the space behind the camera.

One president marries his office, then goes out, then another one goes in.

He's married to the idea of family values, abstinence, protecting the border.

His State of the Union lacks existential questions.

Something about sun.

Something about summer and a lake and Frisbees trimming off edges of sky.

Something about how the hawthorn tree caught air inside it.

Something about clinging to youth.

There's always something above you and below you, forward and behind, and I can't quite
    isolate what is actually where you are.

Marriage: a statue of a horse on a distant hill.

Marriage comes forward like a horse.

Clouds roll in and out like Fords.

I read about the difference between art and endorsement.

I read about the difficulties of absolute power.

I read Martin Buber and think how his picture is like a stone.

Sometimes the things you read recede behind a face in front of your face.

I'd marry that, you think, but not that.

I'd live in there, you think, but not there.

I'd live in there, like an electrical impulse or a socket.

I'd look around. At times, buildings are trees, indistinguishable from one another because
of what is behind them.

In the last thing you say, you say how light marries packing materials, how it marries a
danger-scraped manhole.

You say, "This is somebody's art, not mine."

I see the difference, and it's like for a while I do feel bad.

Disintegration: Poems For Eliot

(IMAGE)

Here is an image for "flag," for "drop cloth for the days I live," for "daughter," "daughter
    like daylight," like "day lilies burning holes in the ground" —

Or here, an image of an attic door hinging open, sounds drifting down as dusty light.

More so than excellence there was an image of buttoning a shirt or slicing an apple into
    white sickles.

There was the precursor to speaking, jangled notes of birds beyond vines.

I am very new today. You, a clean white shirt hung up with pearl snaps for eyes.

(MYTH)

The body whole is a boat of hope-filled pilgrims,

numinous, numerous. Inside a woman, a dark

hole around which she rotates. Inside a child, a tiny film

of sun inching an arc across air. The little

face is a windmill. Little lungs, a pair of tissue-paper

gulls, dipping and falling. Bleached sail, bleached crooked

wings. In endless quiet, words are ruins rising.

An island bruises space. A person throws a gravestone

over what lies behind. In crowds, a body is cleaved or

cancelled. In distance, a body glimpsed. Land like this

must be green and laws entirely natural, pieces of

game looking sharply out under trees and sky.

(MYTH)

In the body the brain folds and unfolds like a flag.

The spinal cord is a sentence. A cell, a space station.

An elbow is the beak of a bird. If the arm is long

the bird has an asking neck. If the arm is short

the bird has no neck and the arm is part of the flesh.

The flesh is part of the shore. The flesh is a tropical

paradise, all that this implies. Green eyes,

a pair of gin rickeys propped in sand. Blue eyes, empty

bottles of ink. The bottles may be filled

with blue water or suicide letters. The man

who lives here is the steward of a heart. The heart

is the size of a puppet, which is roughly the size of

an average-sized hand. The hand is like the little head

of a sunflower. The fingers are pieces of smoke.

(ASTRONAUT)

How lovely the "you" who mores

How little we know following them in their pony phaetons through snow
where small feet leave canoes

A series of conversations wherein the goal is to map out a course of study
and measure of skin

Which is not part of what we look at

How little the nothing is curled inside
a colorless rose

Before it is explained in size by a series
of vegetables

As if to say
what comes before us we will consume
after it gets here

The goal post high as wind
should be
high enough

There was enough of me up to pray.

The sound of human failing is like the pulling apart of clouds.

The sound of breath is like the pulling apart of clouds.

It would be more apt to say "one specific one," one with hair a certain color and eyes a
certain color and a preference for a certain type of dress.

I couldn't pin a pair of eyes on you. I couldn't pinpoint the color of your hair.

I had to imagine grey stones in a few inches of water.

I had to imagine a Tiki torch flickering above your head.

I had to imagine an old Ford left on the side of the highway.

There was a light behind the response, an albino glow that lit the words and the
sentiment. It was, quite literally, a light. I had seen it all day.

(MARVEL)

To place you here would be to place you somewhere, not

somewhere that belongs, the long hook of sun, clouds swiveling around it,

slinking animals pressing themselves through grounded shade.

You wouldn't understand traffic or pavements, looking for signs

where leaves got stuck and froze in wet cement

or our rooms, pellucid, our bodies, our words slipping

through steam, words like *come, go, fissures, spills* — the distances between us great

under great arched ceilings reflected on great planes of polished linoleum.

Somewhere else would be better, a movie of redwoods to make the sky work.

I would like to see you, knelt between slashes of light,

unfamiliar seizures, it was a bird switching trees, you can read the sound.

Can you read the sound? I am not so sure anymore, summer fell

off, and you fell asleep, wrote down this sentence in your head

before you wrote it. Right before you put it down, you had everything.

And then you put it down. Who among us understands signs

the way you do, Marvel? Who looks backward with such acuity?

(MARVEL)

To wrap you in skins in the simple fabrics of thousands of years

from now, a skin around your neck. I keep thinking

about the fecundity of your items of clothing, your tools, leathers

curving against the curve of the eye. I have listened for these things

you never knew you knew, and for Marvel. Perhaps boots

instead of barefoot? Slippers? Are you inhabiting space

or is space inhabiting you? Are the feral herbs climbing walls,

are boys in the other room boys or remnants of another place?

Should we wrap your feet in rags? Should you pray? Should you

add another layer? I have been on the phone all afternoon

weeping. I have been reading books about weeping on the phone,

and you've been wearing this for a while, what Marvel wears.

Documenting smells, butter with sweet wives

and an old, weird-looking knife, the one you normally carry —

Do you have a good mirror, something that could be lifted

and pointed toward a source of light? Your clothes are fine

except for the parts where you've started wearing different clothes.

My clothes don't change. The outside is a sweeping shoreline.

(FIELD GUIDE)

Unfolding limbs you named each "want" and language licked

from the inside of your mouth and schismed

breath in front of you so that sun ran a gruff hand over each hill

so that each was a metallic half-ball

and the minarets and rocky kiosks purpled gently

as heat started to compromise and then the thorns

of light fell off in meadowed yellows and were swept away

by your blue attention, a clear crinoline of wind

grabbing at the ecological context of each form and

each animal whose breathing went in and out of its fur and its ribs

were combs underneath catching the bits of air

and its eyes were bowls of water and its legs were

elevators dropped impossibly down from the chests

and in the chests was felt a stirring like the impulse to act

before they acted and the desire to come forward

before lifting first their right foot then their left —

(DISINTEGRATION)

A red tearing sound breaks a thing into being.

The hands so small in your image, the hair so thin.

This heart beats faster than all of the hearts you've ever heard. It is the heart of a mouse, heart of a molecule.

We live in air, I told it, so that it knew how to take a first breath.

Someone arrives with groceries, aspirin, a favor unfolding from a silver car.

Someone has advice that floats through our hair.

Here, where time becomes a bolt of light unfurling.

Here, where long days curled over books break uselessly against the requirements of the hour.

Deposited into my care is this knot.

It looks very like me, only smaller. It has small wants.

It is not proof, but it is the shape of a morning glory.

It's not proof, but a dog unfolds a howl toward semi-soft stars.

No proof, a bright tree burns the eyes and the eyes bear the tree.

(BIRDS)

George Eliot suggests, "We all of us, grave or light, get our thoughts entangled in
     metaphors, and act fatally on the strength of them."

You who are nothing become in the mind

Sticks put up white flags delineate where a new house may exist

I thought they were birds

Nice names for a girl

NOTES

The *Marvel* poems are for Grace and Katie.

The quote from the last poem in the collection is from *Middlemarch*.

My gratitude to *The Boston Review* and The Catenary Press for publishing previous versions of some of these poems. Many thanks to Elizabeth Scanlon and those at *The American Poetry Review* and Copper Canyon Press who have put their energies toward publishing this collection.

Thank you to all the individuals who inspired or provided support for and feedback on these poems and others. Thanks especially to Joanna Klink, Mark Levine, and all my former teachers of poetry, and to those who have been so generous with their readings and discussions of my recent work: Amy Jurskis, Karl Olson, Grace Ortman, Daniel Poppick, Rob Schlegel, Mary Robertson, and Timothy Tone.

Thanks to family and friends for support along the way. Thanks to Eliot Iris and Randall.

ABOUT THE AUTHOR

Heather Tone is the author of a chapbook, *Gestures* (The Catenary Press). Her poetry has appeared in *The Boston Review, The Colorado Review, Fence,* and other journals. A graduate of the Iowa Writers' Workshop, she currently lives in Florida.